Alice Greenough
A New Woman of the Old West

by Elizabeth West

Table of Contents

Introduction

Most people know a lot about cowboys but little about **cowgirls**. The reason is simple. **Cowboys** have often been featured in films and television shows. Most cowgirls, though, led private lives on farms and ranches. In many cases, they did the same work that cowboys did, but they seldom got paid.

However, a few cowgirls became famous. Alice Greenough (GREEN-oh) was one of them. She grew up at a time when the West was changing.

When Alice was a girl, life was much harder than it is now. People made many of their own clothes. They had to wash them by hand. There were no frozen or fast foods. Ranchers grew much of their own food and raised chickens, milk cows, and beef cattle for eggs, milk, and meat.

Changes Between 1904–2004

The United States changed a lot during the 1900s. Compare the country in 1904 when Alice was young and 2004.

	1904	2004
People in U.S.	76,200,000	281,421,000
People in Montana	243,300	917,600
Families with phones	8%	98%
Cars in U.S.	8,000	200,000,000
TVs in U.S.	0	219,000,000

Ranches were often very large and far apart. The nearest town might be 40 miles away. People didn't drive there, because most families didn't own cars. They went by horse. They had no phones, electric lights, or running water. Most **rural** people cooked on wood stoves and lit their homes with oil lamps.

Alice Greenough was ⮂ a famous rodeo star.

Chapter 1

Life in Red Lodge

Alice was born in 1902 on a ranch near Red Lodge, Montana. Because they traveled on horses, the Greenough family kept dozens of them to ride. Alice also fed cattle, roped them, and rounded them up. She developed the riding and **roping** skills that would later bring her fame.

Alice had seven brothers and sisters, five of whom would one day work in rodeos. They became known as the "Riding Greenoughs." Alice later said, "We learned to ride before we could walk."

Ↄ Both miners and ranchers lived in Red Lodge, Montana.

⌒ On a ranch everyone—even the children—had to pitch in and help.

Ranch life was busy. The family planted, grew, and harvested crops. Cattle had to be rounded up and fed. Someone had to tame the horses and teach them to carry a rider or pull a wagon. In addition, the fences needed fixing, and the buildings and machines needed repairs. Men, women, and children sewed clothes, chopped wood, and cooked food. Days started early, often before the sun rose above the horizon. In busy seasons, Alice would start work as early as 4 A.M.

In those days, rural people had their mail delivered by mail carriers who drove horse-drawn wagons. Alice's father, Ben, was a mail carrier. Alice helped him deliver the mail. Sometimes Alice would take over the route herself. Alice learned a lot on that route. She learned about horses and about working for others.

Alice said that her father influenced her life. Ben Greenough was an **orphan**. He traveled from New York to Montana at age 16 and hired on as a cowboy.

Ben worked with cows and horses for the rest of his life. He didn't like new inventions such as cars. Alice said, "He couldn't even turn a key in an automobile." But he never lost his enthusiasm for horses.

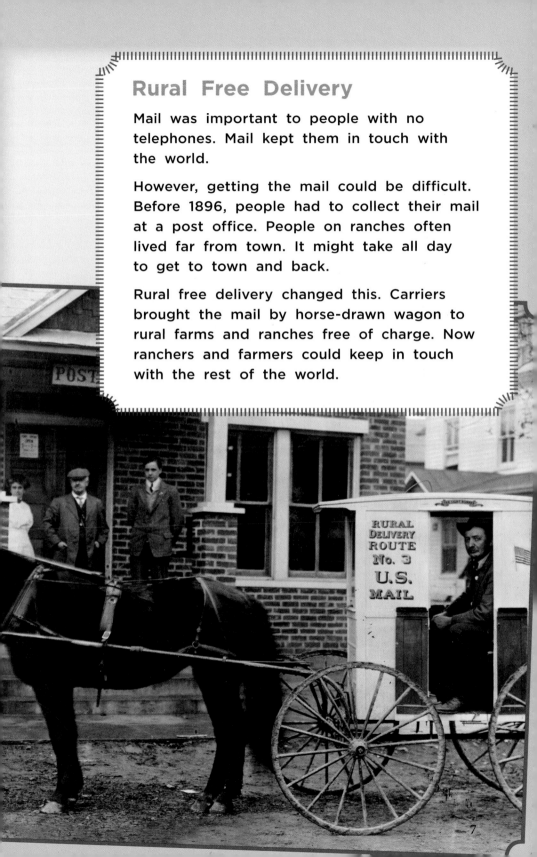

Rural Free Delivery

Mail was important to people with no telephones. Mail kept them in touch with the world.

However, getting the mail could be difficult. Before 1896, people had to collect their mail at a post office. People on ranches often lived far from town. It might take all day to get to town and back.

Rural free delivery changed this. Carriers brought the mail by horse-drawn wagon to rural farms and ranches free of charge. Now ranchers and farmers could keep in touch with the rest of the world.

↑ Alice's family stopped in camps like this one.

Alice enjoyed her childhood. She loved riding, hunting, fishing, and her freedom. During the summer, the family would leave the ranch in the care of ranch hands and stay in a camp at a mountain lake. "I can't think of a day in those mountains that we didn't have fun," Alice said later.

The children held contests to see who could catch the most fish. They had races up a mountainside or down a ravine. They owned fewer clothes and toys than most children have today, but they had far more freedom. The open land of the West was their playground.

When Alice was a teenager, she got her first job. A rancher came to the Greenoughs' house looking for help. "Take Alice," said her father. "She'll work just like a man." Alice was the only girl on the crew. She worked hard to fit in and keep the job.

She also started riding in local **rodeos**. These weren't formal shows but chances for local people to show off their riding and roping skills. Alice and her sister Marge both took part.

Alice mostly rode in races. A few times, she rode bucking **broncos**. When some cowboys brought over a wild horse, she simply climbed on. The horse tried to buck her off, but she stayed on.

↻ Like Alice, Fox Hastings, a famous rodeo cowgirl, rode bucking broncos.

Chapter 2

Wild West Shows

One day Alice and her sister Marge saw an ad. The Jack King Wild West Show wanted bronco and trick riders. Wild West shows were a popular form of entertainment.

⌒ William F. Cody, called "Buffalo Bill," made Wild West shows popular.

Most Wild West shows had rodeos, trick riders, and **sharpshooters**. They also had singers, wild animals, and displays about Native American life. The most famous shows had hundreds of performers.

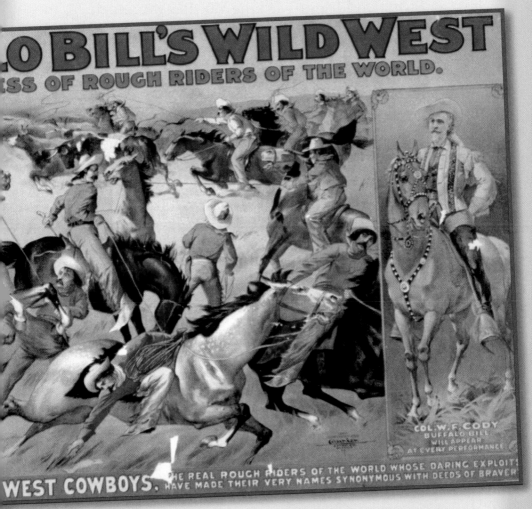

⋒ Wild West shows were popular for years in the beginning of the 1900s.

Alice and Marge answered the ad. Soon they received a telegram saying they were hired. The young women told their parents that they were leaving the ranch. Their parents were upset at first. However, Alice never swerved from her goal of seeing the world and working outside the ranch.

Alice and Marge had not seen much of the world. Now they were off to Ohio to join a **traveling show**. They sewed their own costumes on a hand-driven sewing machine. Motels didn't exist then, so they often slept in tents. But Alice loved her new job. She became an important presence in the shows.

⌒ Alice and her sister Marge perform in a Wild West show in 1935.

Another cowgirl, ↻ Tad Lucas, tips her hat before the World Championship Rodeo of 1936.

Alice and Marge only earned $15 a week, but Alice said they lived a good life. The cowboys and cowgirls were like a big family.

Alice's favorite shows were in New York City's **Madison Square Garden**. At the start of the bucking bronco event, Alice would climb on a horse's back. It would start to buck, often seeming suspended in the air. She tried to hang on for eight seconds, when a buzzer would ring. The crowd loved Alice.

People in New York found such shows thrilling. "They appreciated everything we did," said Alice.

Chapter 3

Ride 'Em, Cowgirl!

The West was changing. The vastness of open, unfenced land was disappearing. Cowboys and cowgirls were becoming a thing of the past. Rodeos and Wild West shows were a way of bringing back that glorious past.

Rodeos showed off the skills of cowboys and cowgirls. Audiences watched people ride, rope, and tie up cattle. The best riders, including Alice, won many prizes and became big stars. Strangers would approach Alice on the street. Some of them had odd ideas about cowgirls. "Where's your pistol?" they would ask. They thought every cowgirl carried a gun.

◔ Many people think that rodeos began with the Mexican vaqueros (vah-KER-ohs). These were the first cowboys in North America.

🎧 Roman races were thrilling to watch.

In the early rodeos, men and women took part in the same contests. Performers were often hurt or even killed.

Alice herself had a bad accident. She broke her ankle at a Texas rodeo and almost lost her leg.

Rodeos started to change. Many closed or became smaller, and they dropped the most dangerous women's events.

Rodeo Events

- **Barrel racing:** Riders race around three or four barrels, circling each in turn.

- **Bronco riding:** A rider tries to stay on a bucking horse for 8 seconds.

- **Calf roping:** A rider chases a calf, ropes it, and ties it up.

- **Roman races:** Riders gallop around a racetrack standing on two horses at once.

15

In 1929 the country entered the **Great Depression**. Huge numbers of people were out of work. Running a rodeo was very expensive, and money was scarce. Many owners had to shut their rodeos down.

Luckily, Alice met a rodeo producer from Spain. He was putting together a new show that would open in Spain and France. Alice decided to go.

A Cowgirl's Gear

From **bridles** to stirrups, cowgirls had a lot of gear. They wore split skirts or pants. Their boots had tall heels that kept their feet from slipping through the stirrups.

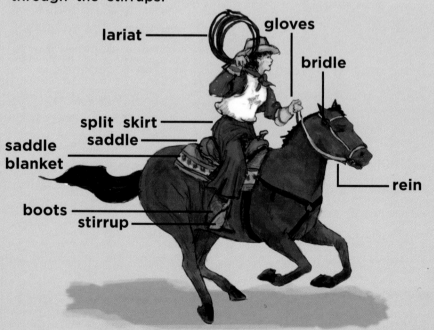

lariat

gloves

bridle

split skirt

saddle

saddle blanket

rein

boots

stirrup

↻ Alice rode bucking broncos. She earned prize money if she won.

The nighttime stars had flickered over Alice's head in Montana. Now, the lights of Europe shone above her.

Alice found that Spain was very different from the United States. At that time, Spanish women seldom went outside alone. One day Alice went out in her rodeo costume. A group of schoolgirls passed her on the street. Their teacher made the girls turn away. She didn't want them to see a woman in pants.

Famous Cowgirls

- Prairie Rose Henderson was known for her bronc riding and for her fancy costumes.

- Lucille Mulhall, called "America's first cowgirl," was famous as a roper.

- Eloise "Fox" Hastings was best known for her **bulldogging**. She could wrestle a steer to the ground.

♠ Cowgirls line up on their horses during a rodeo in London in 1924.

Alice also went to France and later to Australia, where she won an international contest in 1934 and again in 1939.

Alice won contests in the United States, too. Over the years, she lost track of all the shows that she had won. She said that she and her sister Marge worked in every state except for Maine, Vermont, and New Jersey.

By this time, all the riding Greenoughs were well known. "We had a lot of fans," said Alice. "Little kids in school would pretend to be us when they'd ride their stick horses. . . ." Alice met many famous people. She even had dinner with the mayor of New York City.

By 1941, however, most rodeos no longer had women's bronco riding. Fewer rodeos were held. Years later, Alice suggested there were fewer rodeos because there weren't as many "ranch-raised girls."

But western movies and TV shows were growing popular. Alice taught the actress Dale Evans how to ride. Evans and her husband Roy Rogers starred in movies and in a television series. Dale Evans became a famous "cowgirl."

⋒ Television shows about the Old West were very popular. Cowboys were usually the heroes. In most shows, cowgirls did little but look pretty.

When Alice was 39 years old, she and a good friend, Joe Orr, started the Greenough-Orr Rodeo Company. They produced rodeos for more than a decade.

In 1975, Alice was the first person named to the Cowgirl Hall of Fame. In 1983, she was named to the Cowboy Hall of Fame. When she was in her 70s, she told an interviewer, "That rodeo life was a good old life."

↺ Alice was the first person named to the Cowgirl Hall of Fame in Fort Worth, Texas.

Conclusion

Alice Greenough lived through many changes. She started a museum called the Carbon County Museum. It holds an amazing collection of papers and photographs of her rodeo family.

Today, women rodeo riders are viewed as athletes and not curiosities. Alice was one of the first professional women athletes. She helped expand the horizon for women everywhere. She helped to change attitudes about what women could do.

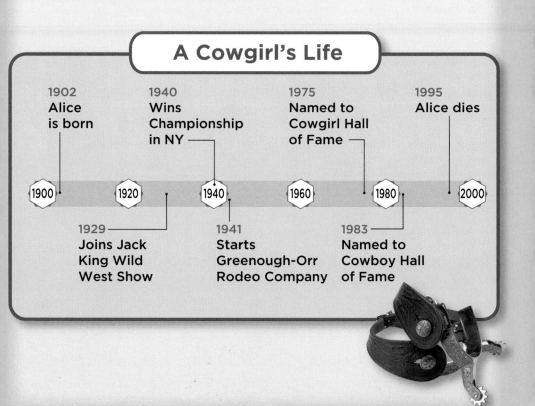

A Cowgirl's Life

1902 Alice is born

1940 Wins Championship in NY

1975 Named to Cowgirl Hall of Fame

1995 Alice dies

1900 — 1920 — 1940 — 1960 — 1980 — 2000

1929 Joins Jack King Wild West Show

1941 Starts Greenough-Orr Rodeo Company

1983 Named to Cowboy Hall of Fame

Glossary

bridle *(BRIGH-duhl)* the straps, bit, and reins worn on a horse's head and used to guide it *(page 16)*

bronco *(BRONG-koh)* a wild horse *(page 9)*

bulldogging *(BUL-dog-ing)* wrestling an animal to the ground *(page 17)*

cowboy *(KOW-boy)* a boy or man who works with cattle and horses *(page 2)*

cowgirl *(KOW-gurl)* a girl or woman who works with cattle and horses *(page 2)*

Great Depression *(GRAYT di-PRESH-uhn)* a time of economic hardship in the United States that began in 1929 *(page 16)*

Madison Square Garden *(MAD-i-suhn SKWAYR GAHR-duhn)* a building in New York City used for large events, such as circuses and rodeos *(page 13)*

orphan *(AWR-fuhn)* a child with no parents *(page 6)*

rodeo *(ROH-dee-oh)* a contest in which cowboys and cowgirls use their skills *(page 9)*

roping *(ROHP-ing)* using a rope to catch an animal *(page 4)*

rural *(RUR-uhl)* in or relating to the country *(page 3)*

sharpshooter *(SHAHRP-shew-tur)* a person who is very skilled with a gun *(page 11)*

traveling show *(TRAV-uhl-ing SHOH)* a group of performers who travel from place to place *(page 12)*

Index

Comprehension Check

Summarize

Summarize Alice's life. Tell why and how she became a famous cowgirl. Explain how her early life helped her prepare for her career as a rodeo star. Use an Inference Chart to help you combine text clues with what you know.

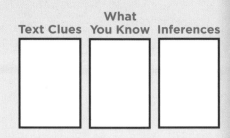

Text Clues | What You Know | Inferences

Think and Compare

1. Turn to page 4 in this book. What words show that Alice was skilled with horses at a very young age? **(Make Inferences)**

2. If you could perform in one of the rodeo events mentioned in this book, which would you choose? Why? **(Apply)**

3. Western movies and television shows are still popular today. Why do you think that people still enjoy seeing shows about the Wild West? **(Evaluate)**